Footnotes

Avik Chanda

Footnotes

Shearsman Books
Exeter

Published in the United Kingdom in 2008 by
Shearsman Books Ltd
58 Velwell Road
Exeter EX4 4LD

www.shearsman.com

ISBN   978-1-905700-67-7

Cover photo and design: Barun Chanda.

Acknowledgements
Thanks are due to the editors of the following, where some of these
poems first appeared: *Shearsman, Stride Magazine, Orbis, BrittleStar,
Other Poetry, Borderlines, Sentinel, Coffee House Poetry, Comrades,
Dogma, Richmond Review, Spork, Octavo Review, Blackbear Review,
Adirondack Review, Rearview Quarterly, Eclectica, Reflections, Morpo,
Aesthetica, The Allotment, Envoi* and *The Queen's Quarterly.*

Contents

For my parents

Postcards

You have laid them out on the table
like a pack of cards,
white reverses facing upwards.
The pictures (which I cannot see)
are the world and its faces,
jagged colours, its pieces of history.
And I draw a card thick with
evening and emptiness
seeping the old quarter, the trickle
of people thinning along winding
concave cobbled lanes
the leaves a rustling vortex
from nowhere to nowhere, with
only the streetlights coming to life.

At the Breakfast Table

for M.B.

A film forms over my tea –
cracks sprout at first, then tendrils
echoing the texture of a leaf membrane
in silent discrete segments.

Observe each further
and the pattern repeats, so now
you see dark clear water, flavoured
and frond-edged: the peace coast.
And a child playing by the beach
who will not come home.

His silence bleeds like a teabag.

Memorial

A figure hunched in the silent rain.
Bandage or blindfold around the taut skull
light reminding what the body had endured
lashes, blows and bits of rope
cutting through starved skin, touching bone.
A single carved head, lowered for many.
Now write their names:

Bernhard Fladderack
Jan Johannes Frikke
Alex Kortum
Josefa Paplowitsch
(V)ladimir Snihur
Simon Zoelle

Und fünf Unbekannte
Ermordet in April 1945
Durch die Gestapo.

A storm gathered and it was dark.

Then three children appeared out of
the night, came and stood
before the figure. Their faces had
the look of petals and the scent of rain
they opened their palms and light
shone through, warm and whole
spreading around the square
then there were voices and the dance
of feet on cobbled stones and
laughter and music and light.

Venetian Sequences

I
At first, there's nothing but the breaking
of his song through the fog. Then, expectant,
you allow first light into this scene – and
the gondolier appears, arms spread out
in mock drama, rehearsing a part to his fare
of Japanese tourists. The gondola passes
in slow motion. The quay, quiet once more,
postcard-like. Now call up the fog again.

II
Recycled souls of men who faded in dungeons.
Now pigeons haunt the chessboard piazza,
drawing shallow shadows in a pattern
that mirrors the water's lace.
Churchbells and wingbeat create their
own music, mingled with voices real
and imagined, as the four horses look on;
then the light swells, whites out everything.

III
Close–up. A man, middling, comfortable at
his writing desk, shirt open at the throat,
sea in his glasses. Paper & pen. Stillshot.
Distracted, he looks up, away from the camera.
Cut. Then, what he was looking at.
As I write this (over an indifferent coffee),
seated amidst music and a teenage crowd,
the real city, far away, breaks into verse.

Souvenirs from an Italian Shop

for Joydeep

Pigeon feet under the eyes of my dream,
where the piazza draws its hypotenuse
of sun and sunburn on faces and breasts
and a waitress whose lips are demerara,
selling softies to the accompaniment
of lace-crust and the rustle of epaulettes on silk,
supplying the movement of a heavy torso
its touch of mint. Nearby, an old balustrade,
peeled, reveals flowers – a late blossoming
of obsidian, red against a black age.

Squads of rain and light. The memory of a night
sculpted in colour and water – and the water
in turn all skin, tethered to its native decay;
and a light, another, tracing a benign palm,
its shadow freshly painted on two coats
of wet plaster. Then the light passed
and the shadow flaked off the wall, bringing

the visitor to a vision of a crowded wait,
cans and food-packets still held, half-empty
and hasty, misaimed kisses as the train approached.

The Cathedral

Two right hands draw an arc
over stains of wet glass-bottoms,
fingers inching to a meeting
half way across the table.
I look up from the smoky light

and Cologne looms above, darkling,
tangibly cold. And a voice
that says: I am the shape
of all things to come,
two hands joined in prayer.

Night in the Schatzkammer

St. Engelbert – recumbent, heavy with
gold and the passing of centuries,
having seen the back
of another tourist-staring day,
slides the weight of his chin
along the hand, stifling a yawn:
all forty seven wounds
still intact and gilded.

The same routine now for ages.

He looks up. Directly overhead,
a weightless glassy space –
beyond, between the V of spires
rises his vision of the sky,
complete with soggy blotter clouds.
And on sudden nights like this –
the drumming
of thunder, Beethoven-like,
splitting Cologne in slices.

Nostalgia. Or call it the wish
to be alive again, that
fetches the old memories
sharp as a nib.
His fondness for words
and swords and crusted viziers.
Power, the servility of men,
and in draughts,
stilled candle-smells
still praying at the altar.

Humayun's Tomb

Each time you close your eyes,
you look up a sheen of swords.
Where their hilts meet, light climbs
the palm of the dome;
pigeons animate an irrevocable time.
Then a swarm of horses casts
after-images on your retina,
surrounding the façade stone-scratched
with heart-signs and lovers' names:
you hear their hooves in the wind's ear.
The arches bend and grey like
the king who sheltered here when
everything was lost, thinking:
in this place, I shall be safe,
my spirits will protect me.
The breath of guns and traitors
swims up like shapes in the heat.

Now you may open your eyes:
they are all still there.

Flashback

for Bando and the others

Muffled rumble of stage-props in the wet dark,
as unlisted inchoate adjustments reshape
themselves in the wings
into a new version of reality.
Then curtainrise and you're borne again
into giddy light and Nineteen Ninety Four.
Young and forever different, arriving
repeatedly at the same spot, indifferent
to your changeling existence.
Nothing tires one out so much
as the sense of time passed, unused.
And each fresh year returns blebs
to brown the reminiscing celluloid.

Memory rewrites itself. *Give it time.*
I stare at Bando when he says this.
The moment passes –
and then we digress. Not the breathless
rake-like anticipatory thudding, then,
or my raving over absent heartless sylphs,
nor even the waiting, but *giving*.
That one and lonely unrequited verb.
Like a litany returned. Or airy light
bursting in with ropy yellow mote-beams,
as Bando reassesses
the sloping bluewash anaesthetic
of his room, shifts in bed, allowing
the needle to assume an easier pose
in his arm, sighs and says: *Give it time.*

Altarpieces

1. DETAILS FROM THE MARRIAGE FEAST

What St. John glosses over is the aftertaste
of middling wine, an uneasy hubris
spreading exhaled alcohol murmurs,
insatiate in the dark overheated hall.

The governor of the feast sweats through
his own raging thirst, scans
the drunken haze for prey or meat
and wiping his palm on the robe,
snaps two choppy fingers for more.

Whence the truth hits home –
They have no wine.

So the action unfolds backstage, where
Jesus, cool and sleek-haired,
stands in the umbra of
his own inchoate congealing glory.
Stands and waits before the casks.

Reddening the water, like blood, becomes him.

2. Night in Galilee

Arranged loin-clothed on the bed like
a foreshortened Mantegna –
Christ, asleep.
Leper-mouthed pilgrims, doubts and
the two Marys tiptoe across his dream,
which thereafter draws a blank.
Nothing and Everything
resemble each other like the faces
of twin mirrors assessing the sea
from across a stretch of tugging shores.

At his feet, thick incense sticks worm
their magic into the clammy dark peristalsis
their scented memories collecting
ash and the dust of a mourned star
once the compass of shepherds and wise men.

At dawn, he will wake to find the world
changed subtly by his dream.

Small Interior, with Dustbin

A single-bed, lit where three beams
pond in, betrays shades
bald spaces the penumbra
of things clinging like memories
to where they once have been,
a congregation of possibilities
converging to a no.

Counterpoint. A dustbin, frog-headed,
sits at the foot, its open gulp
taking in the refuse of lonely nights.

Here, we have once been
and here, the leaves have gathered to stay.

Composition in Blue

An open blueness, as in Miró,
but anamorphosed so that when
seen from an angle, the threads
and microbes dissolve, coagulating
into boats rooted at San Agustin,
their stunted masts meshed against
a liquid Majorca moon rising
between the blued and the blue.

Perfect, you think – and turn around
to where an obscenity greets you,
scrawled above the seats near the
sidewalk, smearing the edge of
the canvas where I would have signed.

Passing Through

Draw a line of light in the blue: then
thumbs pressed together along its seam
like nutcracking, open up streets for
abbeys, music, carriages with watery
peopled shadows. And a name: Salzburg.

And on a nightdrive through this name,
the pilgrim shakes off his hooded nothingness
watching the lights mellow to candled out
carbon smells. Seated there alone, watching.

April 19

Later that day, his assistant
was to remark: *He wasn't careful when*
he was walking in the street,
or when he rode his bicycle.
He was thinking of other things.
That, perhaps. Or the rain.

But maybe it was because
he thought death was a
crepuscular symphony, an electricity
the sky poured out in crystals,
that he did not see the horses
and their six-tonne load
as the tool of his end, even
in that instant when the wheels
shut out his light.

Composition in Grey

I arrived as one should, when going
to church, cold and hungry, wet May
raining spears, fire, bombs and radiation
on the dome. And an arrow for Ursula.

Monochrome even to the touch,
the entrance: a door revolves into
its past, the hinge sifting in
time and tense with weightless ease.

Inside, light gathers like wet husk,
clinging to the shape of prayers, sighs,
draughts and coughs spreading like
footfalls in the old chapel.

And I said to myself: in a cold
hopeless hour draped in hurt,
God could choose for himself
a spot like this, to pray.

Postcard from Barcelona

for J.L.G.

The skin of some dreams. Light in the
Passeig de Gracia, silhouetting pedestrians
in blue, liquid verbs. A woman's hair
that lends colour to the sunset.
The stench of a nun disinterred.
Shadows and signs in the Gothic quarter.
Column of concrete resting on a fossil turtle.
Turron. Posters in a café serving stale food.
Sunday that brings a man to God
then out again on the streets,
where he wanders in the naked light
begging for alms, to build a church.

Lines on an Afternoon, Downtown

Coldness set to the shape of C minor
invades you, broods in your helix.
Slant of stray rain. Gloveless, his breath
still bluing in the air, he tames a Polonaise
on his handy portable pianoprototype.
Heavy, wet notes occupy the space
to where shops and people converge,
like optimal values stuck in a system
of looping, floating transparencies.

'You play beautifully.' 'Danke schön.'
Your memory, or rather, lack of it,
now boons him a name. Hauser.
The music touches semi blind-spots,
so that your vision dissolves, reverses –
an old negative exposed to the light,
lightening like distance. Like the horizon.

The only colour in this scene
is the memory of a ruby cough.

Nature Morte

Images and effects passing like slides:
a corduroy pattern that the tyres
had ploughed in the snow. Leaves,
marigold and a disease – packaged
for transference where a road forks.
A jewel on her finger that returns
light to the night lamp. Blue rain
like a passage in a Bach concerto.
A name that escapes me, but not
the eyes that accompanied it.
Finally, a dream in verse, where
a cellular phone rings insistently;
then a plaster cast hand reaches out,
dismissing the man's number
that had surfaced all too familiarly.

Footnotes

It was mostly during the summer months,
when arriving early before class
we'd dart across from college,
ducking under the sun that made
the street glisten and shimmer
like cathode heat,

into a dark building. Then up
the stairs, past the first morning
whiff at the coffee house,
towards the bookshop. But before
that, the room on the left where
he sat, large spaces around him

stacked with books. A proof-reader,
I thought. Or small-time editor:
his white head bent over the text,
adding a note here and there.
Never looking up. Light settling like
the thick dust on his shelves.

And today the heat returns to
another summer, with nothing
but these lines to stand in for
ten years, his white memory,
for our lost innocence.
And all our forgetting.

June 2002

Heirloom

She waits through the silent falling dusk,
sipping from porcelain
that had sustained grandmothers
through winters of waiting –
for their men to return from the war.

The Conversationalists

The conversationalists wait till last night's
whispers have settled on the phone
in wordless, frosty poems – drops in
a vacant darkness – to set the tone.

Then the froth-day erupts, lemon light
spread on water like a fine lace –
and they begin to weave their words
into the light, the flight of birds,
woods and snow and fog
and the forgetfulness of constellations.

Days pass while they talk, and the meadows
sing, colleagues and companions
sweep in and out of roomy, dusted lives,
telephones melt and are replaced,
tea-stained moons sag at the edges
and all along the Rhine, churches
go mad in the ecstasy of their bells.

They have much to parley about.
Love, like a God, can bear
a hundred and eight names.
More. And then, less. So that

it's night, and months have passed
when they meet again to make
an end of it. And each then
retraces steps to an empty bed,
reflecting on what remains
of certain strained memories:

"Thank God the fit is over –
but look how hard he'd tried."

"She didn't love me, for sure –
but still, at least she'd cried."

A Footnote on Cartography

Without wasting words, let's say a child
wasted her afternoon studying scars
on a map pinned-up in the kitchen.
Her finger grazes a river (the wet bruise),
tracing a sleep-thin thought that I
will not deconstruct. And this paper,

magnified, spread out on a table, once
endured a night with finger-stabs, flag-pins,
orders rehearsed, followed by silence;
then an Emperor's gaze, fighting fate,
history and the sickness in his gut.

The child once more. Now grown-up,
who knows and will never again remember.
Observe her tracing of my brow
the thumb closing my hollowed eyes.
Sleep, she whispers. When all words
are spent, sleep is everything.

His Resolve

Only the moon's wave colding the surface
of glass and fibre, undermining any sense
of permanence, as he walked by the building,
its edifice unbrickening with each fluid moment.

A tree leavens overnight. Spring.
Admitted: the concrete's grey resolve,
blotting out the sky, his own darkening
tent seeping, sweeping everything.

The night after sees him driving out
to the frontier of his loneliness,
along the aorta of the bridge to where
it meets the highway, searching for a light
over the curved horizon to bob up, to go into.

From the Site of the Blast

I

'People were running. Their bodies
were burnt. I rushed out of
the shop, stopped some taxis
and helped the injured into them.
At the hospital, it was the same –
people were lying outside.
Some were dead. They kept moving
all the people who did not show
signs of life to one side, away from
the entrance. I saw at least
fifteen to twenty bodies kept aside.'

II

"He wanted me to photograph
him feeding the pigeons. Then there was
a deafening noise and I fell to the ground.
I don't know how long I lay there
before I finally got to my feet.
My head was bleeding and I felt
a burning sensation in my eyes.
I looked at the spot where he stood.
It was all black. Him and the glass splinters
from the *kabutar khana* and the pigeons."

III

"You're bleeding, here – lie down." ". . ."
"Where are your parents?" "I don't know."
"Where are you from?" "Flames!"
"What's your name?" "Flames all around."
"Are there others in the shop?" "I don't know."
"Lie still." "I need my mother."
"Let me bandage your face." "I saw her in flames."
"How old are you?" "Nine."

Mumbai, August 25th 2003

Mumbai, August 25th 2003

Mumbai, August 25th 2003

Mumbai, August 25th 2003

Casablanca

Each rerun is like an old love, reviewed
where during commercial breaks, one sips coffee,
flashing back to passages of a private script
inserting a description of evening to gloss over
an indiscretion. And with this emerges the idea
of selflessness made credible, as when
you realize certain loves are redeemed
only once you've let them go. As with Bogie,
when he thinks 'for all of us.'

The Reader

White-hooded paperbacks on display
like a deciduous landscape
dressed and buckled for winter.
Thinking not of him, but rather
of what may stand in for time
and a frosted absence, she hesitates
then goes in and buys
herself a volume of Rilke.

Still waters. Still thinking, she walks
down a windswept street onto
the open where a river surprises her,
stops, smiles and opens a page
white as the torpid Rhine
waking in a bed of thawing suns.

Untitled

Remembrance. Time drips
off its rim like rain
around yellow streetlamps.

You're now lighter
than a language
that speaks only to itself.

Barabbas

Rereading Lagerkvist, I turn the page
to where Barabbas, finally freed
from his fear of death, would die.
Guilty of his need for faith.
He follows the others in a procession,
unchained. Glosses over
the face of the crowd. Lingers.
Then ascends the cross.

Two-Euro Coin

Obverse

inclined, to let the sheen outline
his tell-tale cape, laurels bracketing the cap –
the lambent Dante-profile long dreamt of,
that dreams in turn incessantly.

Reverse

His exile. No verses here – only
the number in an outsize font,
indicating commerce in varying
shades; which suits us well,
being only shades ourselves.

Divinities

Cupids, even the grotesquely fat ones,
inevitably show off when photographed,
waving flowers and curls, lips puckered
in a daintier-than-stucco pout.
Angels, however, are a different matter.

Waiting through an eternity
of distant sculpted smiles, in torpor,
black or broken winged, ripped in turn
to bare shell wounds or the scourge,
they bear the mark of Cain.

There are those in hiding, darkly,
till the floodlight bursts in on them
from atop a crowded monument – and
for an instant you see the beaten profile,
an eye iris-less, where acid had lashed the face.

And those living among us incognito –
the girl you asked for change
at the railway station, feeling
the brush of light in her fingers –
whom we are yet to discover.

Legacy

Unbend the time, this unceasing span
of our mutual solstice. Lie still.
Unbraid what we have, to bring
the coils loose, inspect and capture
the rupture in our words. Assume nothing.

I ask again, and you retreat,
thickening your silence to a wall.
I press, and hear a soft gurgle,
of you weeping, lapping against
the shores of my question.

Ours, then, is the stuff of tradition -
books and poems on winter afternoons.
Not for us the quick or the vulgar
but rather the tortured languid fever
that tarries and will not go away.

Years later, they will extract the tapes
to discover a garble of words,
our voices joined and inextricable,
verses read backwards, your tears
in reverse. And understand nothing.

Fording the Epics

And since we're only taking turns
at myth-nibbling, imagine for a
moment you're the fish –
kept alive by teleology,
in an artificial covenant,
but waiting to be struck down;
and over all the centrifugations,
your mind stalking an image
of immortality reached only
through the eye of an arrow
striking your eye.

– from the Mahabharata

Nabami

I
Heat, during the day,
the view shimmering
as if seen through flames.

The leaf that twirled
into my palm
burns in the sacred fire.

Wood and cloth crackle
where fire and water meet;
sand rustling. Dissolve.

II
Incense and the dance of lights;
The priest, swaying to the beat of drums
wakes in his dream, to the Goddess,

lofty and unapproachable,
and therefore alive – a smile
visible through the smoke.

Hands that have held me
now fold in prayer.
Cut to

III
The night. Longshot.
Echoes of drums
silent in the distance.

The city, dimpled with pandal-hoods.
They throw off
parabolic nets of light

into the sky, focii meeting
at a point beyond –
Three-Eyed.

Of Mirrors

yatha bubbulakam passe yatha passe maricikam
evam lokam avekkhanatam maccuraja na passati
                The Dhammapada (Chapter 13, 170)

Having overcome my initial fear, I strode
onto the slippery surface: or rather, was led.
Nimble steps over her own reflection, she was
my fairy-guide to her garden,
once even clasping my hand tight, lest I fall;
fish gleaming under our feet in hurried streaks.
And I, being impure, had thought all along
the glass was water.

Right in the thick of it,
so that now the sea surges up from all sides
in puissant spikes. Then seasong
played fast forward and amplified
in your ears, while a wave freezes
overhead in mid-shock, yawning an open
gulpy palate. Limply, your face
hangs over it, concave in reflection.

A touch – and the spell is broken,
stretched over the foible till the elastic snapped:
shards spread on the void, the light
still knocking off shines along the edges.
Bending, you see pieces of you and her,
scattered, reminding how you have
walked together, now fragments
too numerous to collect.

Celluloid of the Sultan at Play

Here's your scene: longshot in sepia
closing in slowly – the light is atonal,
dimly revealing another evening
after court, except where the film
has worn away and phosphoresces
in patches at the corners.

The nobles, accustomed to converse
in turn through signs and panegyric,
are silent tonight; intoxicants, may I add,
are forbidden by divine decree,
for one never knows what sedition
wine might breed.

In the background, a girl dances
swaying to the policed music
her sweaty torso visible in glazes
beneath the veil – dances till her
strength fails, a heady ribbon of carbon
poised to be extinguished.

Histories

I
Wood a million years old,
long timed to stone, now lying on its flank
in an empty porch, where on
undisturbed afternoons, crows perch
to spread their chalk. And to think
I almost fell off it once,
as a child, tightwalking its length.

II
From here, you hear the guide saying,
you only see the tip of the palace.
Underneath, the king's favourite
dreams up her body as a lake,
blue to the touch, and the light,
festering at the surface,
plays in her vault like shoals.

III
Footfalls in an old lane. Rain washes
down a slope towards the building.
At the entrance, a gargoyle,
leper-mouthed, screams inaudibly
at the unexpected visitor,
who hurriedly folds his umbrella
and steps into the dark.

IV
A moment of sublime distraction,
when, as in that ancient dusk,
the Tirthankar inhabits the smile
in his own bust,
but only for a moment,
leaving the stone
vacant and blind like a child.

V
And to feel that I am all these
and many more, older things –
swords, armies, dust in sunlight,
a stone in rigor, carved
and polished to perfection,
in turn broken, but kept ticking,
waiting for oblivion.

Love-Piece

Dipping my face in your reflection,
I execute a kiss from the love-text,
my darkness merged in your outline.
I lift my face. And the water
has drunk, hollowed your opalescence.

And must we try again?

Knowing that the mirror, now frozen glass,
cannot braid you away in ripples
like before, in scattered shafts –
shall we walk the fog again,
testing our feet on the lake?

Desert Island Disc
for Patricia

Late summer afternoon. A path
along the Jas de Bouffin, painted
by Cézanne at a soaking perspective
of greens. The trees distanced to light.
Somewhere a bird is singing,
lending the painting its open breeze.

You can't see the bird.
But the strip of yellow light
breaking near the horizon
makes you believe it's there.

Rain-Fugue

I
It is raining today, for two people.
The patter – patterned to discern discrete
conversations in the spread umbrella-tops,
the already forming puddles in street corners,
in cobbled stones made to look old –
leaves images in the ear like snatches of dialect,
hurried and brusque, if a trifle indiscreet:
staccato insinuations that do not perhaps matter.

II
It has been raining all day, for two people.
There is nothing else. And everywhere,
their smell, indoored, trapped like stagnant water.
The sky lowers its tent of nimbus, declaring
another dark. Already the April at home
has simmered to a point that makes one
go mad. Or fall in love. In the unbearable
heat of home, too, it is raining.

III
I've made up my mind not to speak,
or to speak only when there's music playing
and the memory of loved ones descends
in a muted twilight, a grey polyphony
more comfortable than the days
we fill with emptiness, calling it 'space',
with a truth that is over and out.
We have decided not to speak our minds.

IV

Then, after all this silence, the rain.
This wet quiet was an ambiguous peace –
and we braided it, holding the combed sleep
like masks before our faces, eyes averted,
till the moment passed and we relaxed again,
the terror of our inevitable grey inward looks
shallowed by the water, now etching branches
across the pane liquidly with its nib.

V

Speak to the dead. They never spit back.
Or to those waiting to die, to see the skies pour,
alternating incantations in semi-consciousness
with dreamt conversations with others, dead
or dying. Or me. Always the dead are with me,
between the two of us, walling our mutual distance.
The rain all day had been a kind of solution,
almost like something we could cling to.

Independence Day

Some ponder endlessly over ephemeral things
meaning to extract some meaning,
to make a statement. And to say that
if a droplet dribbled from a ceiling
above this portico at the Victoria Memorial,
it constituted a metaphor for ways
of looking at the Empire, lost. But not for me.

It was mid-August that year
and I was in love so all that mattered
was the smell of rain and your skin, mingled,
and the feel of broken light
spreading at our feet, against the backdrop
of a sulphurous sunset.

Today, I felt that again (failing)
and how differently it spoke to me
and to you, perhaps, not at all.

Torch Lamp Drawings

I
A neat triangle at first, equilateral,
as in the Vastusutra, then another,
inverted and superimposed on it,
and at the bottom, craggy letters
in Bengali: fire, water, life –
the desperate refusal of hope.

II
Thin strokes strung in a mesh
around the wishing tree: Puri.
Here, for a hundred or two,
we guarantee riches and sons
and a laptop job. Tie your string,
my good sir, like the others.

III
Lively at the *Nacht der Museen*:
a clot of mellow light at the top
left-hand corner, with lines
sliding down in beered perspective,
tracing a lithograph tracing Böll:
der Zug war pünktlich.

IV
Dermis over veins, blood, flesh
and metacarpals. Her hand.
And between the sunburnt here
and there of skin, this most
delicate of all strokes, marking
the band where she wore her ring.

Rembrandt Papers

I STUDIES OF THE HEAD OF CHRIST

Here's a man I found in the Jewish Quarter.
Cultivate him. He could be Jesus.
Some notes, while we're on the subject:
A. No highlights behind the head,
offsetting the profile against wormed
wood, no haloes. B. The ochres tinted to
sallow skin, the shallow forehead.
C. A hint of oil in the hair – touches
of lead white, to scrape or blend later.
D. Slash the brown in his robe, the white
fringe soiled, as if He were scourged already.
E. The shadows under the eyes deepened
like a dark passage in the synagogue.
F. I repeat: the eyes must say everything.
G. Jesus was – and should be painted as
a Jew – and I don't care how Rubens saw Him.

II RETURN OF THE PRODIGAL SON

For this my son was dead, and is
alive again; he was lost, and is found.
                        – Luke (15, 24)

I come to you with sapphire eyes
blue crystal and red gold,
in your death;
in strips of lead white, bleeding,
in long-lost memories
feeding on your mind
till you are mine.

You are my prodigal come home
my diseased lines in stylus;
you are silver against the plate
glistening like fish-scales –
inert, till the acid bathes you.

III DEATH RIDING A HORSE

alias the man-on-a-horse watermark
in his drawing sheets, X-rayed
so that its ghost transcends
the caricature, approaching the infinite
which defies all forms

The Waterseller of Seville

Pathos in drops of water
amidst the heat. So when
the ribmarks on the pitcher
have nearly dried,
choose the tender dark shade.
And a subtle brush.
Stains trickle down. Evanescing.

Like tear-shine on your cheek
at dinner – expended,
then brushed away. Now
I look into your eyes again
and find my cup empty.

Conversation in White Minor

Somewhere in the firmaments, today –
a crackle of lightning
that was not there in the script.
The Dow Jones jumps up, shares heave
and sigh, their graphs
snaking in craggy fugue and anti-fugue
chartering the market's response
to a moment's flicker in the sky.

The music of the stock exchange
does not appeal to us. Landscapes
and locales melt to a still-life.

London, Brussels and Cologne dissolve
through three years
to our favourite stock-reel: the café
overlooking a cobbled old-town square
ten yards by ten, with pigeons
in its centre, courting spot-lit, and
a barrel organ playing off-screen.
In the elsewheres. My voice
stroking yours where it trails off in sighs,
naked forefinger caressing your hand
as if searching for freckles
amidst the whiteness of sand.

Malevich

I
In the end, there was only white.
The canvas, too,
stripped to its bare minimum
frame
perfect square.
Three coats of paint, opaque,
smooth as skeins.
In it, garbled forms dance
shapes that are dreamed of
that do not exist
streams of infinite colours
reaped by phosphorus

II
And how would I ever,
having reached this,
what is certainly a dead end,
return?
And how shall I
make virtues of dead blocks
stolid buildings
purpled distances lined with blue
the colour of loss?
To paint figures again,
women aged before their time
pregnant, starving,
but always falsely muscular
always these ridiculous fists raised.

III
Then there were the nights
while wind and ice raged outside
like tortured stars.
In bed, disarranged
over the sheets
the eyes that could still speak
know still the value
of what had been lost.
A late photograph.

IV
Praised be the absence of content over the
Praised be the absence of colour over
Praised be the absence of consciousness over the
Praised be the absence of shape over

                  There shall be no texture
                  There shall be no form
                  There will be no

V
In the end, there was only light.

A Drawing by Leonardo

This is a final statement showing
the statement cannot be made.

A girl, sketched in rapidly, points
towards something outside the frame,

to what cannot be seen, so that one's
gaze passes from the print

to a table, to books and a coffee cup.
His joke is impeccable. And therefore

the smile on her lips is his
own – having seen what cannot

be wrought in strokes or
calculations or the Euclid he

knew so well, he chose for his
subject a vanishing point

where art passes over in silence
to let all smiles meet.

Postscript to an Elegy

When we die, it will not become darker.
It will, perhaps, grow lighter.
                                        – Anna Akhmatova

Admit it. Already your memory of him has
faded like the sheen of cellophane,
evanescent, on dusty photographs.
The dust rises and falls. Time thickens.
Leaves lie in a heap – and like corpses,
shudder and cringe when burnt.
The dead lie, sure that they will be forgotten.
I think only the dead could endure that.

So what remains? Of his voice, that temper,
the feel and smell of aged, hoary skin
folded onto itself? His raucous self?
Whole afternoons spent in the sun and shade?
And, oh – the endless, endless stories . . .

On recluse, unprotected nights, the fate
of his late years returns
to haunt you. The ebb of a man,
forced by others, and you,
to be let, and then left, utterly alone.
And with it, an account heard obtusely:
him, amazed at the rage of his pain
that surpassed his own rage,
sitting up through the night
of his end, swearing that there is no God.

Memory-Triptych
for Ulrike

I
In a comparison of infinities, God,
my chief obsession, takes first place –
and so my churchgoing in Cologne.
I have not seen my own Gods.
Yet, between the aisle and the altar
between the organ and its codex
I have spotted His Old Testament-profile
primeval and dark like a draught
forbidding and unforgiving
like so many of my own.

II
A 2:30 a.m. moon. Winter light.
Walking in the snow. The silence
of blue crunch phosphorescing underfoot.
At the crossing, dwarfing the traffic lights
a strange translucence in the sky, that
had the feel of morning windscreens –
cold and crusty: a rub of the thumb
would produce a crack, the wipers
clear the frost, and I look
through it, beyond the void.

III
You, my empfindliche late October,
you *were* there (and here I speak of
the present as if you were my past),
my andante sunset, as when
the violinist tunes his instrument,

creating a note that is not part of his score
and therefore transcendental – you were
my moment when the Gods had withdrawn,
after granting a spell of off-season snow,
and only the pain remained, my thaw.

Time

The ancients have told us
that time is an illusion.
The idea is simple – to wait,
wristwatch in palm, as the plane
traverses continents through fog
and light, and at the announcement,
adjust the hands in jerky calibrations
of truth. Night changes to morning.
Or whatever. At which point, the sun
disintegrates, cracking its dials on
aged plinths and a lone chariot wheel
at Konark crumbles under phantom hooves,
brittles, mellows, turns to crispy light,
leaving behind no shadows to count.

Beginning the Century

F Sharp

here no note is heard
only a feeling
that precedes time
moment before the word
had been formed
the unsaid remains
the now

G

then the great questions
now that our world
has come to an end
why does a new light
break the crusted cold
pink like a smile
and what if
all our journeys
ended to question vacantly
our learning again to believe
and what if

A

the new world arrives
on winged truths
caped in winter light
and all our dreams

of a hundred years
rise like a prayer
from our diseased existence
say the word now
say it now and be blessed

hope

– after Sibelius' Second Symphony, Allegretto

Les Adieux

for Shikha

Adagio – Allegro, ma non troppo

Waking up before time into the prospect
of departure and a blank ceiling,
I can think only
of the loneliness of wharves
in the greying dawn. Memory of
spot-lit, chain-smoked spaces
soggy consolation of nights
in some decrepit pub.
London in frost like
a crust of confectionary.
Light on still water like a second skin.
Immobile pattern of a flock of birds,
white, on the skimming mirror of water,
like an array of smoky frozen foam.
I concentrate my energies
on such emblems of stillness.
And so the hours drip by, outside time,
like a dreamy Ravel,
towards the sun. Checking the time,
finally, I call for a cab
and run my eyes over the place
for a last stocktaking.
A sunlit pint still sweats on the sill.
Moon under water. The moments spill.
Daylight worms through a page
of poetry on the table,
mellowing the words away till
all that remains is a watermark.

So it happens that this midwinter morning I'm seated
in a spacious cab, plumed and kitted
like an exotic bird – or like Murat in full blossom,
all colour and glory, leading his cavalry into the sun.
A penny for your thoughts of valediction.
The taxi driver, originally from Lahore,
is a natural philosopher, generous with his words,
sprinkling Urdu poems along the route he chooses
so that Clapham inherits Momin, Osterley – Daagh,
and Hounslow - the pensive nazms of Faiz.
Great poets, all. Dead poets. All gone into the dark.
And there is now only the past to comfort us.
And oh! How things even back home have now
degenerated! Follow the West, follow the West!
That's the brandished motto of today's youth –
down the headlong, sure slide to perdition.
And here, in this grey vast city, there's no love –
people exchange names in bed
and change names and beds the next morning.
We keep the conversation lively
but as the car nears Heathrow,
he frowns at me through the rear-view,
switching suddenly to his English:
"So where you're going – Bhaisaab?
Where is your home?"
And had I been Ghalib, I'd have answered him
with a wan curl of the lips and a ready sher,
saying that though a horse had been prepared
for the journey and you had a foot in the stirrup,
the course to the Kaaba was still unknown;
but I can only smile in reply, wishing there was a name
that could answer to the notion and feel of "home".

Adagio affettuoso

Having seen off Patricia at the terminus, I am
suddenly gripped by an attack of melancholia
such as I thought had long been abolished.
Minutes slacken and perish. The bus trails off
into the scorching heat. Dust kicks up
its chorus of silent detritus
into the early autumn of loneliness
and newly-harnessed buses spew out their fare
of tanned tourists in wide-brimmed hats,
maps and guides and mineral water.
Only the sun can make such poetry
out of this indolent dust, rising and failing.
Clearly, there is nothing left for me here.
Alone again, I pass the afternoon
stalking the haunted geometry of Jaipur,
its silent decay, burnt colours of a history
too glorious to be reinvented. And then stand
before a ruined fountain,
filling my hands with sand.
Someone has been waiting for me
among these ruins.
Eyes and a voice behind a veil.
Whose – I did not know then.
And so it seemed to me that one could
only hope to arrive at her portrait
the way the truth of a complicated function
searches for its meaning
(ingress of an orb of light into
the impossible looping darkness),
to be at one with its own converging limit –

but only in the end,
the way time sheds its old skin
on another age rife with heat and strife
and stars spill their perfumed dust
in sequins on a dark veil,
the way the veil too, lifts, amazed –
but only in the end,
in the soul of waning colours
whose dusk is their own reply.
The veil lifts thus from your face.
And men, with wounds that blossom,
approach your fragrance as pilgrims
offering incense and
the burnt sienna of memories.

Andante molto espressivo

Les Adieux. With Napoleon at the gates,
its characters enact an aristocratic dance,
rustle of silk and movement of a trance –
as in a masque: Rodolphe & Co. seated at table
with eyes that do not glance
and lips that do not pray
each face wearing an expression
(reflecting the bleakness of the day)
that can only signify defeat and an imminent exile,
while musicians assemble unhurriedly in a corner,
spread out their sheets and begin to play.
In the background, swords and currency
are hoarded, crockery shudders
and jewels gleam in hastily-shut boxes
while the scene converges to a close-up
of lacquered hands and red knuckles
carving anxious knives through the meat.
But the music continues throughout this departure
so that the notes grow tumid, droop and liquefy
on melancholy strings - but still manage to comfort,
sheets of music float in their languid moodiness
without dropping to the ground – and thus
a movement emerges on its own, thoughtfully,
accompanying the slow-motion of carriages
into the wet lilac of misting distances. Exeunt.

Adagio molto – Allegro vivace

Goodbye for now. These ruminations in the half-light,
to put it loosely, are your inheritance. Yours, then –
these pieces of borrowed history, solitary walks
in the rain and fog through half-deserted streets
or tales of loves past, like dead rubies
soaked in brooding amber. Fingers curled
around a flame that nourishes and burns.
Lines glisten when written, while the ink rides them,
then subside and remain what they are:
merely an effort, in moments
of self-importance and pride – or pain,
to gather and preserve fragments of feeling.
It is time now. The ink congeals.
Dust gathers in the corners of unturned pages.
The poetry creases and ceases to matter.
We read on. You say that nothing
would remain of my metaphors. I agree.
Words Are. Till such time that poetry happens to them.
Words, like music, can move us. And shadows
may form smiles on the lips of marble saints
in ancient cobwebbed church-corners
that men have forgotten to worship.

In passing, then, it is this instant that I shall talk about.
Now, as day breaks again outside this cathedral
of unlit memories, it is Sunday and summer –
and so it is that instant again – at home,
in India, or London, or perhaps the draughty moment
in the Kölner Dom, where all is dark
and the Chorale ascends and haunts the vault

like a moth fluttering in an overheated room, frantic,
crashing into arched lights, in search of an open window;
and then ineffably a light passes over your eyes
and rouses the walls of the cathedral; and a man
who journeys across the waters with a child
stops and bends his smile towards you.
And then a ship passes, spilling lights on the wine.
And everything is at once made lucid and kind.
Today and here and now is that moment.
This, however, no longer remains my poetry.
Let me leave you now. For I shall open
the hinges of the past and step out into the street
like a child waking into a new summer of lights.